Church, Bride and Wife

Church, Bride and Wife

MIROSLAV HALZA

authorHOUSE®

AuthorHouse™
1663 Liberty Drive
Bloomington, IN 47403
www.authorhouse.com
Phone: 1-800-839-8640

First published by AuthorHouse   10/04/2011

ISBN: 978-1-4670-0161-8 (sc)
ISBN: 978-1-4670-0162-5 (ebk)

Prologue

According to the story of Creation, "a man will leave his father and mother and be united to his wife, and they will become one flesh" (Genesis 2:24). Traditionally, Jews call marriage "sanctification," because it involves a spiritual bonding in which a husband and his wife are perceived as one soul in two bodies.

The Disciples witnessed this divine precept in the person of Jesus, the Son of Man and God. Christ Jesus himself declared this sanctification during the Feast of Dedication, by saying, "I and the Father are one" (John 10:30). In fact, God in Christ Jesus wants to apply this divine precept to all people. "*Father, just as you are in me and I am in you, may they also be in us*" (John 17:21). Our Savior wants to have such a relationship with everyone coming to God. This precept is the final state of our relationship with God.

The final state of ordinary human relationships, at least between man and woman, is marriage. To reach to this state, a couple first becomes engaged; then they must go through a wedding ceremony, and after that, they can finally dedicate their lives to each other. Those who partake in each stage are called specific names: for example, a young man and woman are a fiancé and a fiancée throughout the engagement. The wedding ceremony makes them the groom and bride; then, the husband and his wife live as one flesh during their marriage.

Our relationship to God is very similar. First God, in Christ Jesus, found us and redeemed us. We became his Fiancée. Later a wedding will take place, and we will become His Bride. After the wedding ceremony, we will be His Wife.

This transformation of the true believer from Jesus Christ's Fiancée, to His Bride, and finally to His Wife, is the subject of this book. The book's arrangement follows this outline:

1. Introduction
2. Church
3. Bride
4. Wife
5. Conclusion

Introduction

God the Father has chosen His Son to populate God's Kingdom. His Son must be God; and thus, He is God the Son.

In his Revelation, the Apostle John saw the Heavenly Throne and its Occupants. Hence, he had to see both God the Father and God the Son. The Son is He who is performing the will of God the Father. In relation to the events of the Last Days, God the Father wrote His will on the Scroll, and has given it to His Son to act upon (Revelation 5:7). From the description of He who took the Scroll, it is clear that He too is God. He must be God, because He stands at the center of God's Throne. As beings must have both body and spirit, so it is with God.

The Apostle John saw the Spirit of God as the Seven Spirits (Revelation 4:5). The body of God the Son looked like the Lamb, having seven horns and seven eyes (Revelation 5:6). The Bible declares that the Seven Spirits of God are in His eyes, and therefore there could not be any doubt that the Seven Spirits are the Spirit of God the Son.

As Eve was created from Adam's rib to bear children for him, so God the Father had to take some part from God the Son to bear children for Him. Christ Jesus tells us this was the Spirit: "I tell you the truth, no one can enter the Kingdom of God unless he is born of water and the Spirit. Flesh gives birth to flesh, but the Spirit gives birth to spirit" (John 3:5-6). Thus, the original population of the Earth is born from the water of an internal reproductive organ (the womb), and the new population of

Heaven (the Kingdom of God) is born of the Spirit. Two separate births are required before one can enter the Kingdom of God.

The Kingdom of God has at least two stages, according to the places of realization: they are the Kingdom of God on the Earth, and the Kingdom of God in Heaven. Hence, the beings in the Kingdom of God could be partly Earthly, and partly Heavenly now; or just Heavenly then. What is partial should not be full, which is why our relationship to God can only be partial now, but will be full later on, in Heaven. The perfect metaphor taken from the Earth is this, then: now, on Earth, each of us is like God's Fiancée; later, after entering Heaven, each will be like His Wife.

To be a fiancée means to be promised in marriage. Christ Jesus gave us this promise; and therefore, the first ones receiving this word were called Christians in reproach to the followers of Jesus. The body of Christ's followers is known collectively as the Church.

The Church

The Church is the body of believers in Jesus Christ, whose members will be the partners of God in eternity.

If the Apostle John saw Jesus outside the Throne appear as the Lion of the Tribe of Judah, the Root of David (Jesus as the Resurrected Man), and then on the Throne as God the Son (the Lamb having seven horns and seven eyes), he also had to see the body of believers during their progress.

In relation to our theme, what John saw first in Heaven was the Spirit of God the Son—the Seven Spirits, per Revelation 4:5. Christ Jesus was not present, and certainly none of the resurrected men; humans cannot be physically present in Heaven without Christ Jesus while Creation exists. When believers die, they are not resurrected today, and so they are not full beings. A large gathering of these spirits, being many and without bodies, might seem to represent a sea. They are righteous, and therefore the sea is clean and clear; clean, transparent waters can resemble like glass. Yet they are spirits, so some distinctions should be evident among them; thus, the term "crystal" better fits their gathering.

The Apostle sees gathered spirits immediately after the Spirit of God, which should lead us to conclusion that they are connected. First they were tied by a spiritual umbilical cord, because the Spirit supplies their needs to grow while waiting for Resurrection. The term 'born from the Spirit' is what brings them together. As children are naturally drawn to their mothers, so the gathering of human spirits is drawn to the Spirit of God the Son.

The 24 elders and God the Father are described separately. They are tied to thrones, or the power to rule. The One is on God's Throne, and the 24 are on the thrones of heavenly beings. The 24 elders derive their authority from the authority of Him Who sits on the Throne, because they fall down before Him and lay their crowns before the Throne and praise Him (Revelation 4:9-11).

These are the princes, the first ones among servants of God the Father. They must be primary servants of God the Father, because Christ Jesus (or God the Son) is not present among them at that time. The power of these high-positioned servants hinges on the power of God the Father Himself. Their duty is to do the Will of God the Father; that is why they stand in the presence of God (Luke 1:19). The duty of human spirits, however, is to perform the Will of the Spirit. That is why "No one who is born of God will continue to sin . . . He cannot go on sinning, because he has been born of God" (1 John 3:9). If man in spirit does not sin, then others may know that he is born of God. The testimony of Christ Jesus thus exists in our world. Revelation should remain in the terminology of the Gospels, and we should understand that when the birth of human spirits occurs, it is an era of Christianity.

Christians, these who hold true to the testimony of Jesus, are the offspring of the Spirit. But what is the testimony of Jesus? As Jesus demonstrated, it is based on the transformation of water to wine, something he performed from the start of his ministry (John 2). According to the Old Testament vocabulary, God presents bread and wine to His people, so that they may be His beings forever. Since we wait to become the way Jesus Christ is now, we must be resurrected. We will enjoy not just the eternal spirit, but also the eternal body. These realities should be pictured in the second room of the Tabernacle, because people (Levites) entered the Sanctuary.

We use a table as a firm stand for putting essential things upon. Thus, the Sanctuary Table could be considered a tray for valid holy items. Moses made the table, its pitchers and bowls for the pouring out of offerings, the plates and dishes, and put the bread of the Presentation on it to be before God at all times (Exodus 25:23-30). The matter presented on the table is bread, and therefore they called this tableau the Showbread table. What does this bread represent? What do we need for life in Heaven?

We may analyze the eternal stage by looking at the resurrected Christ Jesus himself. His dead body was not left in our world (although it was composed of Earthly elements) but was simply changed, because the Disciples could recognize him as their Teacher (Luke 24:39-43). Something caused the change. This something should be seen in the aforementioned bread. This is because the Lord Jesus Christ "**took bread, gave thanks and broke it, and gave it to them, saying, 'This is my body given for you; do this in remembrance of me'**" (Luke 22:19).

The Church does this. Extreme teachers explain it literally: that Christians receive Christ's body during communion, that the bread is transformed into flesh. However, the true intent is to remind us that the body of Christ Jesus was the same as our own. We should remember that Jesus had Earthly flesh which was later changed into eternal flesh. Although we too are now in Earthly flesh, someday believers will be resurrected into eternal flesh. God, through Christ Jesus, will put some "nutrient" into our flesh that will make our bodies eternal. Certainly, this is for the case of the Rapture (1 Thessalonians 4:17).

But to live eternal life, it is not enough to have eternal flesh. We also need to have eternal spirit. In other words, we need something that will change our souls into eternal spirit. Moses did not put this other matter on the Table; nevertheless, a close look at the Table reveals empty vessels for holding liquid (Numbers 4:7). Why are there empty jars on the Presentation table? Because *God has already poured out His spiritual substance for our eternal spirit.* Thus, we are now already partly eternal beings in our Lord Jesus Christ. We are also able to live life according to God, as Jesus Christ lived.

Jesus told Martha, "**I am the resurrection and the life. He who believes in me will live, though he dies, and whoever lives and believes in me will never die**" (John 11:25-26). It is clear that he spoke of having eternal spirit already during life in the flesh. According to His Last Supper, the symbol of this eternal spirit is wine. "**He took the cup, saying, 'This cup is the new covenant in my blood, which is poured out for you'**" (Luke 22:20). Here, the wine in the cup represents the ACTUAL COVENANT.

Thus, bearing the testimony of Jesus means having a living spirit. This is the NEW COVENANT. The result of the Atonement performed by the Lamb of God is this: human beings may have their human souls already changed to eternal spirits, while their Earthly flesh will be changed to eternal flesh later.

Christ Jesus was the Son of Man. This means that he was the first human being who had a living, eternal spirit in mortal flesh. Therefore, to bear the testimony of Jesus on Earth is TO HAVE A LIVING SPIRIT. No one could achieve this result "**until the Son of Man has been raised from the dead**" (Matthew 17:9).

The Disciples followed the Lord Jesus Christ in forming the new generation on the Earth. In this way, they bore the testimony of Jesus into the world. Therefore, it is not just the life of Jesus that testifies that he was born from the Spirit of God, but also the lives of his followers, who testified they too were born from the Spirit. They represented living examples of the new class of human being. Therefore that world called them "Christ's Ones," which developed into the word "Christians." Christians are not just propagating words, news or theories, but propagating new life rooted in the Spirit of God the Son. Therefore Jesus said, "I am the true vine and my Father is gardener." You cannot "bear fruit unless you remain" in him (John 15:1-4).

The Last Supper compares Christ's blood to wine. Blood carries oxygen and nutrients to the tissues so that life may continue. Similarly, some liquid must circulate through vascular system of a vine. It is a watery solution of sugar and minerals.

The watery solution related to the vine, sugar, and human nutrition is wine. So we may conclude the pictured "wine" is that which holds us alive in God. We must now take "wine" to bear the testimony of Jesus.

This is why Jesus began by changing water into wine and finished, at the Last Supper, by showing that "wine" is the blood of the new generation.

The original spirituality of humans emerges from the water of the female internal reproductive organ, and so from a woman (Eve) whose substance was taken from the man (Adam). This spirituality bears inherited features of both parents—even the original sin of Adam. The new spirituality of humans emerges from the Spirit, which is "taken" from God the Son. This spirituality bears aspects of Jesus Christ's life on the Earth, and even the eternal life. From there, it is only a small step to also have "woman" bearing children for the Kingdom of God.

Revelation 12 introduces "Woman," who gives birth to those who bear the testimony of Jesus. The first one born from her is Christ Jesus Himself (Verse 5). The last ones might appear prior to their snatching from the Earth up to Heaven. Christ comes first, and the whole assembly of newborn ones afterward. Christians associated together are called the Church (Romans 16:5; Colossians 4:15). Hence, the Church is the body of all bearing the testimony of Jesus. By replacing "Woman" with "Church," I conclude that the Church ends with the Rapture at the described place (clothed with the sun, with the moon under her feet).

The Lord Jesus Christ told his followers on the Earth that he would leave them and then return for them, to introduce them to his Father in Heaven; then they would be with him forever. This relates to the chain of man and woman. The links fitted into one another are: fiancée → bride → wife. But while the Word or Engagement runs, as the Gospel says, Christ and his Fiancée do not see each other for long time.

When fiancé and fiancée are separated, under normal circumstances they will correspond regularly, especially as the day of wedding approaches. Similarly, the Lord Christ Jesus sends seven different letters to His Fiancée, the Church (Revelation 2-3).

The First Letter

Let the title of the first letter be: **Praised are You, O Lord our God, King of the Universe, Creator of the fruit of the vine**. (The titles are taken from the liturgy of the Jewish wedding, when seven blessings are recited.)

With this letter, the Fiancé ensures His Fiancée that He now holds all the upcoming events firmly in His hands: *He held the Seven Sealed Scrolls, which seemed to Moses to be like the seven golden lampstands.* She shall receive new gifts from His Father, because the Lamps are His seals (God's seal shines; see Genesis 3:24). God's gifts are mostly God the Father's through the Holy Spirit. Revelation 1:20 says: "Christ Jesus holds seven Lamps, and they are the seven churches."

So, the Lamps must shine because they are the churches. Therefore, the Fiancé advises her to renew her first love to Him, as the first Lamp has started to shine for her. The members of the Early Church loved the Savior over all else, even to the point of laying down their lives for Him; now it is time for such love to come again, since His Lamps are going to shine on each place (city) on the way toward her.

Since the Fiancé of the Church holds seven stars in His right hand as He manages the seven Lamps, the Church should advance. Because the first praising is for the wine of the Creator, the first Lamp shines mostly to pour *wine* among the people. Thus the newborn Christians begin to be visible. Their advancement must be victorious; otherwise it is not true that the Lord Christ Jesus "holds the seven stars in his right hand." Revelation 1:20 tells us these stars are the messengers of the seven churches.

The tribe Judah represents the Church in the Old Testament. There are these words for the Church: "The scepter will not depart from Judah, nor the ruler's staff from between his feet, until He comes to whom it belongs and the obedience of the nations is His. He [the Church] will tether his donkey to a vine, his colt to the choicest branch; he will wash his garments in wine, his robes in the blood of grapes. His eyes will be darker than wine, his teeth whiter than milk" (Genesis 49:10-12). Now Christ Jesus, by taking the messengers of the Church in his hand, has given them a crown in order to ride out as conqueror until he comes for His crown. In order that these who now use it would not be underprivileged, the Owner of their scepter will take them from the world also (the Rapture). If the Lion of Judah has triumphed (Revelation 5:5), then the Gospel has entered the world through the lion's power to triumph. For instance, L. Moody captured millions of people for the Lord Jesus Christ in his years of world evangelization.

The Fiancé reminds her that the engagement cannot be valid if she will not bear His testimony—that is, the testimony of Jesus Christ. She should not accept false apostles who teach that a believer's spirituality is like that of animals, and that therefore any human spirit does not exist. The testimony of Jesus is personal knowledge of God's name and not the life in spirit according to them. The Lord did not send those men to teach. Hence, they are apostles of a being considering himself to be one with animals; or it may simply be that a being who does not drink *wine*

9

is their master. Were the parents of Christ Jesus mere animals? No. His Father is God or the Spirit of God; and so Jesus' spirituality is spirit from conception. His mother is woman, created from the flesh of Adam, who was created in God's image.

Similarly, the engagement would be invalid if she considers herself to be fiancé and fiancée. Such a contradiction can exist only among "Nicolaitans." Namely, some men teach this: a woman will be resurrected when her husband calls her by the secret name he has given her for their marriage in Heaven (men are saviors of women). They also marry (seal) couples for Heaven, where the husband will live in a polygamous family with all the wives to whom he was sealed.

We tend to conclude our letters by expressing some wish for recipient; and so also do the letters of the Fiancé end, with His blessings for His Fiancée. This is the first blessing: He, in the name of God, promises she will partake in the Resurrection prepared for those who go to Paradise after they leave their mortal flesh. *"To him who overcomes, I will give the right to eat from the tree of life, which is in the paradise of God."*

The Second Letter

Praised are You, O Lord our God, King of the Universe, Who created all things for Your glory. And, *"these are the words of Him who is the First and the Last, who died and came to life again."*

The Fiancé reminds His Fiancée that He is the first and the last in Creation, because "all things were created by him and for him" (Colossians 1:16). Although He died, He was resurrected. Hence, His actions which were first should also then be last; and therefore, as he was resurrected as the first man, consequently the last one having his testimony will be resurrected. "And if the Spirit of Him who raised Jesus from the dead is living in you, He who raised Christ from the dead will also give life to your mortal bodies through His Spirit, who lives in you" (Romans 8:11).

The Lord Christ Jesus has realized that his enemy Satan is trying to hurt the Church. That is why He oversupplies the Church with the Holy Spirit. The Holy Spirit has come upon people, and many have spoken in tongues. This spiritual revival began in Los Angeles, California in 1906. "*I know your afflictions and your poverty—yet you are rich! I know the slander of those who say they are Jews and are not, but are a synagogue of Satan.*"

Please take heed of any theological school not having any respect for the bearing of the testimony of Jesus. The Pentecostal movement outrages them, and they start to teach against the Spirit and against the Holy Spirit by advising a return to the codes. Yet 2 Corinthians 3:6 declares that the New Covenant is not of the letter but of the Spirit; for the letter kills, but the Spirit gives life. The Lord identifies these theological schools as synagogues of Satan.

Some believers during this Lamp died mainly where many Christians were first baptized by the Holy Spirit. They were believers who lived on the Russian steppes, who were later moved to Armenia. If they did not migrate to USA, the holocaust in Armenia caught them. ("*You will suffer persecution for ten days. Be faithful, even to the point of death.*")

The Author concludes the Second Letter with God's second blessing for the Church. She, as the Resurrected One, will not be hurt by the second death. The second death is for those resurrected who never ate from the Tree of Life and never bore the testimony of Jesus, so their names have not been written in the Book of Life (Revelation 20:11-15). "*He who overcomes will not be hurt at all by the second death.*"

The Third Letter

Praised are You, O Lord our God, King of the Universe, Creator of man. And "*these are the words of him who has the sharp, double-edged sword,*" sharper than any sharp words delivered by the synagogues of Satan (Hebrews 4:12).

The Fiancé reminds His Fiancée that He is the glorious man. His face shines like the sun in all its brilliance, and out of His mouth comes a sharp, double-edged sword (Revelation 1:16). Because He holds her in His hand, He is giving her the power to use a sharp double-edged sword herself. She may use His sword for casting out demons or to heal, in order that the world may know more about Him to whom she is promised. He has come closer to her already, since the third Lamp gives Him light on the way to her.

For instance, Smith Wigglesworth of England often used this sword: "*Nevertheless, I have a few things against you: You have people there who hold to the teaching of Balaam, who taught Balak to entice the Israelites to sin by eating food sacrificed to idols and by committing sexual immorality.*" The Fiancé warns her not to defile herself by eating food marked to be someone else, or by committing sexual immorality. I consider this His reflection on the actions of the man claiming to have the power to establish the Kingdom of God on the Earth by means of his offspring. Certainly, he could not multiply his family through many women, and therefore uses a "divine trick" to accomplish this. He blesses couples at their weddings by giving them a juice to drink that he claims it is his literal, physical blood, and candy that is his flesh. Thus, they say, a new race is on its way to ruling the earth.

To use harsher words, I would say that they eat symbolic human flesh, and so they are cannibals, and not any new race for God. Perhaps Hitler's propaganda of the superiority of the "Aryan" race inspired this false messiah to develop a more effective teaching method reaching whole world. King

Balak, mentioned in this letter, could refer to those world leaders who supported the "Aryan" race or support this Unification movement.

Likewise you also have those who hold to the teaching of the Nicolaitans. So, a game husband is savior of his wives continues in the next steps toward eternity. They are saving also the souls of the dead by baptizing themselves instead the dead. Their "priesthood" also has such authority.

The Author of this letter ends it by speaking the words of the third blessing of God's Throne: "She is betrothed to the Son of God, with a white stone with her name written on it, as an engagement ring would be offered for her." (A gold ring, sometimes with an intimate inscription, is placed on the finger of the bride.) If it is a blessing, then it is a temporary offering until the blessing reaches a day of realization. As I see it, Christ Jesus gives things of the Kingdom of God (perhaps the land) to whom He is engaged, and so the engagement ends here. *"To him who overcomes, I will give some of the hidden manna. I will also give him a white stone with a new name written on it, known only to him who receives it."*

The Fourth Letter

Praised are You, O Lord our God, King of the Universe, Who created man and woman in Your image, fashioning woman from man as his mate, that together they might perpetuate life. Praised are You, O Lord, Creator of man. I think, this blessing in the Jewish liturgy is the human reaction to the Engagement described in the previous Lamp. *These are the words of the Son of God, whose eyes are like blazing fire and whose feet are like burnished bronze* for the period of the Fourth Lamp.

The Fiancé introduces Himself as the great Knight. If He comes to use His power, His eyes are like blazing fire, and His feet like burnished bronze. This is the description of the Being on God's Throne. Thus, He is also the ruler of the created world and universe, and that is why He knows even her deeds, her love and faith, her service and perseverance, and that she is now doing more than she did at first. Her actions in spreading His name and power in the world should be like the latter rain. For instance, large revivals began in Canada in the year 1948, which they called the New Order of the Latter Rain.

Nevertheless, I have this against you: You tolerate that woman Jezebel, who calls herself a prophetess. By her teaching she misleads my servants into sexual immorality and the eating of food sacrificed to idols. Now I say to the rest of you in Thyatira, to you who do not hold to her teaching and have not learned Satan's so-called deep secrets (I will not impose any other burden on you): only hold on to what you have until I come. Thus, the Fiancé advises her to avoid the teaching of Satan's so-called deep secrets, which are spread by a woman.

I believe this relates to the teaching of divine healing, rooted in spiritual understanding. The mortal mind convinces people that they are sick, and therefore they are. But spiritual understanding is rooted in the changeless Mind of God, where sickness does not exist. Thus sickness is unreal, and therefore should be rejected. A source of divine healing, therefore, is in one's own strength, in one's own understanding. Her primary teaching was developed in a broadly-spread movement called "positive thinking." Thus, positive thinking and faith in one's own ego is Satan's so-called deep secret. "Change your thinking, change your life".

Sexual immorality and eating food sacrificed to idols can refer to practices causing people to have relations with another being or living person. For instance hypnosis, in which one person uses the mind of another person. Brainwashing occurs when someone else's thoughts occupy one's mind; thus, one's mind is nourished by someone else's thoughts. I would compare this to conditioned reflexes in animal behavior. It is no wonder, then, that many practices first try to annul human conscience by cleansing a person's spiritual database. (In Christianity, it is confessing all sins from birth.) A person without conscience acts/is like an animal. Bringing yourself to this stage is like cleansing or washing the heart. So, do you have some problem with your behavior? Clean your database first; become clean in your inner being, as animals are. There is one Spirit (God) for all. When you unite with Him, your desire is on the way to being realized. This is the case with idols. Believers in idols make offerings to them, in hopes that the idols will realize their desires.

The Author concludes the Fourth Letter with God's fourth blessing. This blessing is not preceded by the phrase "He who has an ear, let him hear what the Spirit says to the churches," as it was in previous letters. The Lord speaks straight to the addressed, "to him who overcomes."

I see two possibilities regarding the fourth Lamp. One follows the line of previous blessings realized after passing away, and the second line begins to display the rewards for those who enter the Millennium during their lives. This means that some people must be sealed for the Millennium to start to exist. In other words, some men or women born during the fourth Lamp may enter the Millennium in flesh. If I am correct, then the core of this blessing should have three statements or verses. The first is the naming of the reward, followed by the designation of the first and the second groups.

The Lord Christ Jesus, as Lord of Lords and King of Kings (Revelation 17:14), will give authority over the nations for the period of the Millennium. This authority includes:

1. Providing His chosen and faithful followers a place at His throne, that together they might perpetuate His rule on the Earth. *To him who overcomes and does my will to the end, I will give authority over the nations—'He will rule them with an iron scepter; he will dash them to pieces like pottery'—just as I have received authority from my Father.*

2. *I will also give him the morning star.* A star is meant to be a messenger of a church; thus the Lord promises her the supervision of some community expressing faith in God. Certainly, that person will be invisible for them, like angels (stars) are invisible for us today. This is certainly for those who get eternal flesh in the Resurrection or the Rapture.

In any case, this letter is for a period when the light of the Lamp starts to shine also for Jews (in other words, the State of Israel exists). Therefore the next three letters are in another chapter of Revelation, Chapter 3.

The phrase "he who has an ear, let him hear what the Spirit says to the churches," now concludes this letter. I think the Lord wants us understand that the message of this letter still is for the Church, although Israel is already on world scene. This phrase is in the new verse, and so the fourth blessing extended from one verse to four. Since the Author has now concluded the next letters by reciting this phrase, it repeats four times. Thus, God's rewards/blessings have been included in two verses from the next letter.

The Fifth Letter

May Zion rejoice as her children are restored to her in joy. Praised are You, O Lord, Who causes Zion to rejoice at her children's return. This blessing is a natural reaction to the return of Israelites to their homeland. *These are the words of Him who holds the seven spirits of God and the seven stars.*

The Fiancé continues describing His final image to His chosen and faithful followers. He described His body in the Fourth Letter; now He describes His spirit. His spirit is truly Seven Spirits. They are the Spirit of God the Son, and so His. Seven Spirits should exist on the Earth to nourish believers. The Fiancé dislikes her undernourishing and so words come: *I know your deeds; you have a reputation of being alive, but you are dead.*

The Fiancé rebukes her for just having a reputation, but not being in the right relationship to Him. She uses the gifts gained from their contract to be someone on the Earth, and does not care for own heart (Matthew 7:21-23). Thus, there were no large revivals during this stage. God's gifts are present on the Earth, but they were seen mostly in Christians who are not newborn, do not use *wine*. The Charismatic movement started mostly in Catholic Church, initially at Duquesne University in the USA, in 1967.

Wake up! Strengthen what remains and is about to die, for I have not found your deeds complete in the sight of my God.

Remember, therefore, what you have received and heard; obey it, and repent. But if you do not wake up, I will come like a thief, and you will not know at what time I will come to you.

Yet you have a few people in Sardis who have not soiled their clothes. They will walk with me, dressed in white, for they are worthy.

She should be aware of those who try to soil the wedding robe and appoint His coming for the Rapture. The Lord's words are a warning, because one such prophet estimated the day of the Rapture to occur in the year 1977. Because nothing happened, his followers started to brainwash people into believing that the Rapture of the Church had already occurred, and therefore, every believer must leave his/her church to become a partaker of the Rapture. The ultimate conclusion of this teaching is that every believer has a wedding robe, although is still in Earthly flesh. Thus, they soil the promised white wedding robe.

The Author concludes this letter with the fifth blessing. She will be His Bride; that means she will be dressed in Heavenly clothes, her name written in the everlasting contract between Him and her, to stand at God's Throne in order that He may introduce her to His Father and His servants. *He who overcomes will, like them, be dressed in white; I will never blot out his name from the Book of Life, but will acknowledge his name before my Father and his angels.*

The Sixth Letter

Grant perfect joy to these loving companions, as You did to the first man and woman in the Garden of Eden. Praised are You, O Lord, who grants the joy of bride and groom. It seems to me that these words salute the wedding procession. Thus, we have arrived at the wedding day. *And these are the words of Him who is holy and true, who holds the key of David. What He opens no one can shut, and what He shuts no one can open.*

The Fiancé announces to His Fiancée that He is going to open a door in the wall now separating her from Him. Yet, as it would not be any "mailman" bringing this letter, the fiancé recites these words, staying behind the door. Thus, the sixth Lamp brings the Fiancé to the door to open it.

What "door" is still not open? Humans should also be eternal beings in flesh; this is our destiny. This change occurs through resurrection after death, or through the transformation of mortal flesh into eternal flesh after being snatched up from Earthly life. Hence, the process is called the Resurrection or the Rapture. In the time of the Sixth Lamp, God will open the door for the Rapture and the Resurrection. Once this has begun, no one can shut the door, and the believers who die after the door is opened will be resurrected without delay.

The words about the opened door should not be overlooked, because the Lord repeats them. *See, I have placed before you an open door that no one can shut.* Therefore, this letter is the last one before the Rapture.

Since you have kept my command to endure patiently, I will also keep you from the hour of trial that is going to come upon the whole world to test those who live on the Earth.

Are these not words about the Rapture prior to the Great Tribulation? These words serve not only as evidence for the Coming of the Rapture, but also as the proof that the Church will not suffer the Tribulation.

I am coming soon. Does this not refer to the Second Coming of the Messiah to the Earth?

Hold on to what you have, so that no one will take your crown. The crown was given to the first evangelists, so that no one would take it from the Church. Christians should ride as masters in their triumph. The triumph is that the Gospel will be preached to every nation, and so the Bride will consist of members from all nations. Only a victorious Church could be raptured.

My conclusion is that today's Church is the Church of the Rapture. Pastors should lead followers in this direction. Christians who are going to be raptured feel the Lord's Coming, and ask preachers to speak about it or research it for more information. This is grist for those who do not teach inspired theologies. It is said, "*I will make those who are of the synagogue of Satan, who claim to be Jews though they are not, but are liars.*"

In this context, the term "synagogue" refers to today's seminaries, schools, theological institutes, and other places where Christian leaders receive instruction about the Church and the focus of life in every community. If the Lord says that Satan inspires their instructions, then those teachings may be false in the context of this letter. Therefore, the teachings of present Biblical schools regarding the Lord's Second Coming and the Rapture must be false. Yet there is hope for their repentance, because the Lord tells us, "**I will make them come and fall down at your feet and acknowledge that I have loved you.**"

The reward or blessing overlaps the main message. The Lord promises to his chosen and faithful followers to have a dwelling and working place in the New Jerusalem. *Him who overcomes I will make a pillar in the temple of my God. Never again will he leave it. I will write on him the name of my God and the name of the city of my God, the new Jerusalem, which is coming down out of heaven from my God; and I will also write on him my new name.*

Bride

The Church has the new heart that is in accordance with Jesus Christ (Ezekiel 36:26). It is the promised spirit that ties humans with God. Now, the time of the wedding is at hand. The wedding will be in Heaven, and therefore the Church, as the Fiancée of the Lord Christ Jesus, should first transform, and then move there. From that moment, no one will call her the Church anymore; instead, they will call her the Bride, and the Lamb is her Groom.

A traditional Jewish wedding is a representation of the wedding of God with His people. Several events comprise the traditional Jewish wedding, as outlined below.

Dressing

God dressed Adam by making his body from the dust of the Earth, so that he might live upon the Earth. Consequently, the Creator must also make a new "dress" for the wedding ceremony, if the wedding is going to take place in Heaven. God has another material from which to make the Heavenly dress, according to the Sanctuary's presentation. Moses showed it by placing bread on the Showbread table. Christ Jesus gave bread to his twelve Disciples, and similarly Moses put twelve loaves of bread on the Table. He will not lack any material for this dress, because as Jesus Christ once said, even the very hairs of our head are numbered (Matthew 10:30).

Dressing should take place on Earth, because Christ Jesus was resurrected on the Earth. There was just the single Resurrection then; but now multitudes of humans will be resurrected, and many of them are not in our visible world, but are in Eden, just like spirits. Hence, the Resurrection must take place in Eden, or somewhere else close to the Earth. The Apostle Paul says that we will meet the Lord in the air (1 Thessalonians 4:17). This also means the Lord will push Satan and his servants out from this place toward the Earth, even onto the Earth.

In our society, a maid or matron of honor assists the bride with her dress, and with everything needed for her to be the bride. Similarly, the Church should have a "Woman of Honor" attending her during the wedding. I think the Apostle John envisioned this "Woman of Honor," for he describes "a woman clothed with the sun, with the moon under her feet." If this is so, then the dressing and so Resurrection will take place at least 400,000 km from the Earth.

The Woman of Honor should assist the Bride with her dress. She can tailor the dress to fit her, because She nourished her growth. If this is so, then She takes the material delivered from Heaven and makes new bodies for every spirit, for every human participating in the First Resurrection. During the dressing of the Bride, the Woman of Honor should keep her things, her deeds done by spirit for the Groom. They are her wedding bouquet, made up of palm branches. *They were wearing white robes and were holding palm branches in their hands.* The Bride has palm branches for her Groom, to meet Him with (John 12:13). The Woman of Honor should also assist with the Bride's makeup, because the Apostle John saw Her as having a crown of twelve stars on her head. In this context, stars refer to the messengers, and so should also refer to the Apostles. In any case, the Apostles should be distinguished, perhaps, by having crowns on their own heads.

A groom should not come alone to his bride; he should have other men to be with him. Among them is the Best Man. Because the Groom comes from Heaven, His Best Man is the truly the Best Angel. The best angels, the highest angels, are the archangels. Archangels are chiefs among other angels, they stand at the Heavenly Throne.

It seems logical to assume that the Wedding's Best Angel is the angel bearing the seal of the living God. John wrote: *"After this, I saw four angels standing at the four corners of the Earth, holding back the four winds of the Earth to prevent any wind from blowing on the land or on the sea or on any tree. Then I saw another angel coming up from the east, **having the seal of the living God**. He called out in a loud voice to the four angels who had been given power to harm the land and the sea: "Do not harm the land or the sea or the trees until we put a seal on the foreheads of the servants of our God. Then I heard the number of those who were sealed: 144,000 from all the tribes of Israel."*

Although these men are on the Earth, all in Heaven hear their songs (Revelation 14:3).

Transport to Heaven

When everything is ready, the Bride and the Groom may take seats in a cart or a wagon pulled to Heaven. It may be a chariot, or chariots of fire pulled by horses of fire, according to Elisha's description (2 Kings 2:11). The Bride is then introduced to God the Father.

"I looked and there before me was A GREAT MULTITUDE THAT NO ONE COULD COUNT, FROM EVERY NATION, TRIBE, PEOPLE AND LANGUAGE, STANDING BEFORE THE THRONE AND IN FRONT OF THE LAMB. They were wearing white robes and were holding palm branches in their hands. And they cried out in a loud voice" (Revelation 7:9-17).

23

Jesus Christ redeemed people from slavery and, as the Lamb, has brought them into His home. It is as if He is marrying a captive woman (Deuteronomy 21:1-12); she must wait to see whether she will be accepted in His home. Therefore, the Bride salutes God the Father by telling Him her fate depends upon His Mercy. She cries to Him as though her life is at stake: "**Salvation belongs to our God, who sits on the throne, and to the Lamb.**" The Bride's salutation should be answered; a move by God the Father in her direction is to be expected. Because God is the Highest Ruler and Judge, we may anticipate His actions as a judge—as He views the victims of the world's crimes.

The Bride and the Groom are not alone before the Throne. They have assistants, angels. Because the duty of groomsmen was once to guard a bride during the wedding, angels step to her side. They declare affirmation of what the Bride has said: "**Amen! Praise and glory and wisdom and thanks and honor and power and strength be to our God for ever and ever. Amen!**" Angels are witness that the Bride has acknowledged God the Father and His Son to be her Saviors, and thus has broken any ties to her previous parents. (In a sense, her previous parents have died, and she does not mourn for them anymore.) The angelic words *Amen, Amen* affirmed what she has declared, because they are legal witnesses to this marriage.

Traditionally, a best man would give a speech addressed to the parents of the bride and groom. Similarly now, the archangel takes the next step and brings the Bride's case before God the Father, the Judge. The Bride of the Lamb could not reach God's Throne alone; she is under the veil. Christ Jesus has covered her, by offered blood (Romans 3:25), to be holy. Only archangels, who have seats there, could reach the Heavenly Throne. Therefore, one of those standing before God speaks for the veiled Bride; thus the Best Angel is also the advocate of the Bride.

The censer in his hand contains the prayers of the saints. Saints praised God, provided incense for the Lamb, and were beaten for it by the slave drivers of the world. Such slave drivers, serving Satan, killed many people. Society did not punish these murderers; yet those who were killed prayed that they would be saved. Since only their souls were saved, not their flesh, their prayers wait to be answered completely. Therefore, God should explain why they have received Heavenly flesh, and why others have dishonored their Earthly flesh. Revenge is legal answer. Revenge is the right of all victims. And so, only the punishment of the killers could be a final answer (judgment) to their prayers.

There were many, of course, who were neither able to know God nor to pray; they asked the Creator for revenge because they were not allowed to begin life. These are the unborn babies.

"And I saw the seven angels who stand before God, and to them were given seven trumpets. Another angel, who had a golden censer, came and stood at the altar. He was given much incense to offer, with the prayers of all the saints, on the golden altar before the throne. The smoke of the incense, together with the prayers of the saints, went up before God from the angel's hand. Then the angel took the censer, filled it with fire from the altar, and hurled it on the Earth; and there came peals of thunder, rumblings, flashes of lightning and an earthquake. Then the seven angels who had the seven trumpets prepared to sound them" (Revelation 8:2-6).

God the Father responds. He has accepted her as the Bride of His Son, which He confirms by punishing all who have hurt her. His so doing I would compare to our everyday life; when we see a victim of any crime, words of judgment are handed down for the criminal who hurt them. Therefore, when God receives them (the victims), then He should (according to His identity) judge those who hurt them. If it said, "there was silence in Heaven for about half an hour," then such a period represents a court session. Every punishment must wait for legalization by the court.

Escort to the Chuppah

The bride and groom are escorted to the Chuppah or "canopy" during a traditional Jewish wedding. Joyful music and singing accompany them, because the bride and groom are viewed as a queen and king. The Chuppah symbolizes the couple's first home together. Therefore, after she is introduced to the Groom's Father, the Bride moves from the Heavenly Throne to a place that Christ Jesus, with his groom-angels, prepared for this purpose (John 14:2-3). This is where the main wedding service occurs.

Hence, as the Church moved and left the Earth, so the Lamb must leave the Heavenly Throne to be under the Chuppah. If He cannot continue managing the events of the Heavenly Book, then He should transfer His power to someone else. The Book of Revelation tells us that He transferred His power over to seven archangels ("angels who stand before God"). Trumpets, which are moved from God's Throne to seven small thrones around it, indicate this transfer. These trumpets cause those who sound them to receive God's power; when angels sound the trumpets, their words are as the power of the Lord. They give a loud shout like the roar of a lion, which is impossible for their bodies. Those far from them think that they hear the sound of thunder.

Another aspect also exists here. God the Father appointed His Son to create and to save. Because God the Father now decides to judge, it is better for His servant angels to do this job. Thus, no one can consider Christ Jesus, as the Man, to be the biggest terrorist in history because He lords over the Great Tribulation.

So, the bride and the groom go under "canopy" for the wedding ceremony, and the bride walks around the groom before the ceremony starts, circling him three times. The groom prays while the bride circles; he prays for friends who are not yet married to soon be married. I think that when Christ Jesus is alone with His Bride, He prays first for those who were not raptured, are not with Him under the "Chuppah," that they may join Him before the end of the wedding. There are three periods left for them to do so, since the Bride circles him three times. They have only three periods remaining for them to see Him as the Groom; thereafter, He will be the Lord. Revelation calls these periods "woes." (Certainly, any period so recognized is not for the part of the world which will be destroyed by the First through Fourth trumpets.)

The wedding service starts with two blessings over wine. I believe this represents two kinds of participants in the Bride, as wine is the symbol of the eternal human spirit, according to Christ's teachings. These participants include those who receive the spirit during their life, in mortal flesh, and those who receive the spirit after they pass away (the Old Testament's faithful men and women, or New Testament believers, who did not have the opportunity to live in this spirit during life; for instance, those who lived during the Dark Ages, or were killed before birth by abortion).

The groom places the wedding ring on the bride's finger with these words: "Be sanctified to me with this ring in accordance with the law of Moses and Israel." Then the marriage contract is read. I believe the Lamb will give His hand to everyone during the next period of the Wedding of the Lamb. Perhaps He will give each one a ring engraved with their new name, or put something on each forehead that could be easy recognized as an indication that this or that one is for the Lamb. Meanwhile, others will learn the Law of God, which will be sanctified also by their deeds.

Then Seven Blessings Are Recited

This confirms that they have learned God's Law, and are able to exist in accordance with God's demands. No one in the Old Testament was able to fulfill the Law of Moses completely, and therefore none was a saint while on the Earth (besides Jesus Christ). But this stricture has fallen away now, because new beings will live in accordance with God's Law. Since they are saints because their deeds, they do not need atonement cover anymore. Therefore, Jesus Christ removes His covering from them. In the Jewish wedding ceremony, the groom unveils the bride's face when the Seven Blessings are recited.

Here is the Seventh Blessing, the last one: **Praised are You, O Lord our God, King of the Universe, who created joy and gladness, bride and groom, mirth, song, delight and rejoicing, love and harmony, peace and companionship. O Lord our God, may there ever be heard in the cities of Judah and in the streets of Jerusalem voices of joy and gladness, voices of bride and groom, the jubilant voices of those joined in marriage under the bridal canopy, the voices of young people feasting and singing. Praised are You, O Lord, Who causes the groom to rejoice with his bride.**

Breaking the Glass

The wedding ceremony ends when the groom steps on and breaks a glass. So, the cessation of the Heavenly banquet marks the last part of the wedding of the Lamb because preparations come in the direction to Jerusalem and the Temple in it. I believe this last period will involve accepting instruction on how to manage events on the Earth during the Millennium.

After breaking the glass, the bride and groom retire to a private room to take few moments to relax together. This could refer to taking a private room in the New Jerusalem.

Wedding Party

Finally, the bride and groom return to wedding party and greet their wedding guests. In the same way, I believe, the Redeemed will return to the Heavenly Throne to greet the angels. Now, basically, they are the same beings; they are all God's servants, with the only difference being that angels are servants of God the Father and so the Heavenly Host, whereas the Redeemed are the servants of the Lamb on the Earth. I believe this will be the last meeting in Heaven before the invasion of the Earth (Revelation11:15).

I believe, also, that the Wedding of the Lamb occurs during our dwelling in Heaven. Perhaps because people are in Heaven just for while the word Wedding is used. They should be there during the Seventh Seal. Also, the term 'the Bride of the Lamb' applies for that period.

In order to have a complete picture of that period, we need to return to the believers on the Earth. These are ones who were saved upon the breaking of the last Seal. I would compare them to groomsmen, from the words **"These are those who did not defile themselves with women, for they kept themselves pure"** (Revelation 14:4). They were left on the Earth to guard Home for the Couple to live there.

Since the Creator created during the light of six days, six Heavenly Lamps shone during the building of the Home for the new Couple. The Lamb first stepped up for Creation, and the first Lamp began to shine (Revelation 5:13). He gave His authority to the Church to ride out as conqueror. Their task was to subdue the Earth under the Gospel, to preach the Gospel to all nations. In this way, Christ Jesus has been brought to all nations, and His name was proclaimed over them to accept the coming Creator and Savior. "He came to that which was His own, but His own did not receive Him" (John 1:11). Regardless of the fact that not all accepted His offered Mercy, He has right to come there and to take His own. Now, as the Husband of she who was persecuted and mocked by them (they who cursed Christians and their Lord), it is His duty to avenge her.

These 144,000 Redeemed ones rejoice because of the wedding. "The bride belongs to the bridegroom. The friend who attends the bridegroom waits and listens for him, and is full of joy when he hears the bridegroom's voice" (John 3:29). The final joy will be expressed by seeing them return Home.

Then there are those believers who were not saved at opening the last Seal. These believers did not have mature spirits; according to Song of Songs, they are young sisters who are not yet grown up (8:8). The Words for them are in the Seventh Letter for the church in Laodicea.

The Seventh Letter

"These are the words of the Amen, the faithful and true witness, the ruler of God's Creation." If the Author of this letter introduced Himself as the Amen, then progressive ministries for created beings end by extinction of the Seventh Lamp. This means that no Rapture or Wedding could occur after this letter. Thus the mystery of God, just as He announced to His prophets, is accomplished in this Lamp. Upon the end of the last Seal, Christ Jesus will be the history. He can serve only as the witness of all that God had intended for His people. It is enough for them to be eternal beings and to have God as their partner. They should await nothing else; they will not be gods.

After this Lamp, Christ Jesus will not be the Man, but God the Son, ruling Creation. He will not rule these eternal human beings; they will assist Him as His partners.

"I know your deeds, that you are neither cold nor hot. I wish you were either one or the other!" This indicates that the Rapture must have occurred by this point, because "hot" Christians do not exist when the seventh Lamp started to shine for Earth. "Hot" Christians are these who do not sleep, and have enough oil (Matthew 25:1-13).

In spite of the fact that some Christians were raptured, those left behind might decide that they were fine; they might believe that they had remained on Earth in safety, while the disappeared perished in catastrophes. Indeed, some teachers even teach that 'one taken' is taken to perish, and 'the other is left' because he is righteous (Matthew 40-41). Their understanding of some Biblical texts holds many denominations and Christian groups together. They believe they are right with God, because they hold more of the truth than any others. Thus they are rich in their own eyes, while all others are wretched, pitiful, poor, blind and naked. But God's word of this Lamp shines so: "But you do not realize that you are wretched, pitiful, poor, blind and naked."

Is God so poor that He does not give any Heavenly thing to His children, especially in the period when Christ Jesus, the head of the Church, steps up on the Heavenly Throne? (Colossians 1:18; Revelation 5). Logically, this is impossible. If a believer refuses to accept anything from God, then that believer should not be God's chosen man or woman. The most important thing any Christian can have is the eternal spirit (*wine*) in his or her body. Therefore never say, 'I am rich; I have acquired wealth and do not need' the spirit. The newborn spirit is this thing that identifies you as God's child. Any other understanding, or the pursuit of any revelation of any other person, does not give you legitimacy for the Wedding of the Lamb.

People receive the eternal spirit when they reject their soul habit—their ego. They need to have died in this field, that the new seed may grow (John 12:24). Thus, death is what may make humans truly rich. When

Christ Jesus advises them to buy from him gold refined in the fire in order to become rich, then they should not love their life; rather, they should die for faith in God.

Since the door for humans to become Heavenly beings is open, everyone with the right to become a Heavenly being should immediately enter after passing away. Therefore, the Author of the seventh letter says: **"Here I am! I stand at the door and knock. If anyone hears my voice and opens the door, I will come in and eat with him, and he with me."** They immediately enter the Wedding Supper of the Lamb, thus not the first gathering (introduction) at the Throne. These words testify that the Resurrection has already occurred, because believers from this Lamp will go directly to the Wedding Table. This means that the *Wedding Supper of the Lamb* is occurring at this point.

God will reward those faithful until the Second Coming by appointing them to the new government established by the Lord in the material world. This should apply to those 144,000 who wait for the Messiah in the material world. *"To him who overcomes, I will give the right to sit with me on my throne, just as I overcame and sat down with my Father on his throne."*

Marriage

The Marriage of God the Son with His people represents a revolutionary change in Creation. If one compares the period from the end of the Creation until the end of the Wedding of the Lamb to six working days for the Lamb, then the next Millennium must bring a day of rest to Him.

I speak of God the Son leaving the Heavenly Throne. I suggest that the first task for God the Son was aroused when Satan rose to oppose to the Creator, causing Adam to fall. Because Satan was the first among angels, some higher throne (someone with higher authority) had to step down to replace him. I believe God the Son offered Himself for this task, and from it He bears also the name the Lamb. He became the Mighty Angel. This caused the angels who were displeased with Satan's actions could leave him and turn to the Mighty Angel. For the instance, I believe Michael left him after disputing with him about the body of Moses (Judah 9).

Then He proceeded to show that another prince of the world exists; see the Exodus of Israel from Egypt. The Mighty Angel established the new nation, which was thus God's nation. He lived with Israelites, as it would be their marriage with Him. He was even visible to their leader Moses, who spoke to Him face to face (Exodus 33:11). Other nations could see that God was in Israel; and so they had the choice, still, to either consider Satan to be the ruler of the world (Luke 4:6), or to turn to the King from God's Throne—to God in Israel. This historical state of the world was not progressive, however, because even Israelites left God, who dwelled among them in the Temple. Thus, the people of the whole world continued serving Satan.

It was necessary to redeem people in order to complete the Creation with a good result. Therefore, the Lamb stepped down for His people's sake. He became the Man, who redeemed them from slavery. So that the redeemed would not turn back, He also granted them the possibility of living an eternal life in spirit. And finally, He brought them to His Father and entered in partnership with them through the contract of the Wedding of the Lamb.

His Wife has partnership with God, as Adam had before he got Eve; with the distinctive feature that they are eternal beings, for they have left Earthly flesh behind. They have become purely Heavenly beings, because they dwelled in Heaven during the Wedding of the Lamb. If they are Heavenly beings, then they must have their private rooms there in Heaven. According to Revelation, their new dwelling spaces are in the city called the New Jerusalem. It is not a city built from earthly stones; it is *"the city of pure gold, as pure as glass"* (Revelation 21:18).

Earth's gold is not transparent like glass; light cannot travel through it. Earthly gold, like all other minerals, is a solid material formed in three spatial dimensions. Similarly, gravity causes all habitations and routes to them to be more or less on the surface of the Earth. But Heavenly houses could be built without gravitational effects, thus growing high even as they spread in width and length. Thus, the New Jerusalem would basically have a crystalline structure. "He measured the city with the rod and found it to be 12,000 stadia in length, and as wide and high as it is long" (Revelation 21:16).

The reality of gravity dictates that an Earthly city could not move from its location on the Earth; but such is not the case for the New Jerusalem. Even modern cosmology recognizes that some form of repulsion, as well as gravitational attraction, is observable in the universe. Gravitation links to mass, and the expansion of the universe to *energy*, mostly observable during novae or supernovae.

I believe that the Second Law of Thermodynamics, which denies any evolution, predicts these forces. According to the Second Law, entropy is constantly increasing in the universe. Entropy is defined as waste energy (heat) that cannot be used to do thermodynamic work. Since heat is associated primarily with the vibrant and rotational motions of atoms and molecules, the gravitational force and the repulsive force ought to arise from the decline of the vibrant and rotational energy of atomic particles. In general, vibrant and rotational motion generates both longitudinal traveling waves and transverse traveling waves. Therefore, I believe, these longitudinal traveling waves and transverse traveling waves carry both the gravitational force and the repulsive force (energy).

As I understand it, the gravitational force is the result of the vibration of particles that lie mostly in the atomic nuclei. Protons and neutrons (both baryons) vibrate due to the elastic potential energy they obtain from forming their bonds. Compression due to extreme density, as occurs in the cores of stars, creates these bonds. In an attempt to break free from this pressure, some force pushes them apart. As they try to reach a stable configuration, free from any tension, they are moved toward the equilibrium of their bonds. Their potential energy of compression is therefore constantly changing, and as a result they acquire kinetic energy. They reach their maximum kinetic energy at equilibrium. Since kinetics refers to motion, inertia does not allow them to stop there, and strains the bond between them. And so, they just slow down to the maximal distance between them. As they stop at their maximal extension, they are again at the maximum of their potential energy. The conservation of energy for this system must apply, and so any increase of the kinetic energy must decrease the potential energy (per the First Law of Thermodynamics). It follows that decreasing the kinetic energy—decreasing of the velocity of protons or neutrons—increases their potential energy. In classical physics, their motion is described as simple harmonic motion.

It is reasonable to imagine that certain subatomic particles of protons or neutrons might tear away as their movements slow down upon reaching maximal displacement. Let me name the smallest particle the graviton, since physicists use this term for a hypothetical elementary particle that mediates the force of gravitation.

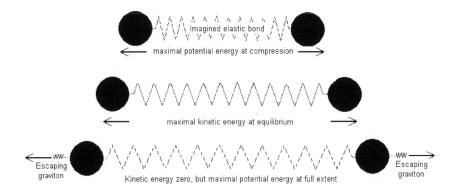

A change in kinetic energy must occur for a graviton to be emitted. But according to the Second Law of Thermodynamics, some energy is unable to do useful work and is changed into heat, which increases entropy. According to German physicist Rudolf Clausius, the entropy of the universe tends toward a maximum. Hence, the natural order of the universe will run spontaneously until all proposed work is done in the universe; thus, entropy appears to be a divine energy provided to maintain work in the universe. All work will be done when this divine energy reaches its maximum and is restored.

Since gravitons ought to be emitted when protons or neutrons slow down on their way to maximum displacement, the speed of the graviton must be less than the speed of the protons or neutrons close to their equilibrium point, e.g. at their maximal kinetic energy. And since we know the constant speed for photons in vacuum (that is, the speed of light), I assume that the speed of gravitons in vacuum is the same, for all kind of gravitons. Certainly, I assume that gravitons are emitted in all directions, due to the rotational motion of atomic nuclei, per liquid drop models of such nuclei.

When a graviton meets a proton or a neutron moving in the same direction and at the same speed, the graviton, due to its familiarity with the particle, should merge with it. As the met particle accelerates (**a**) to approach its equilibrium, the graviton speeds up with it. Hence, the speed at which gravitons propagate through materials is more than their speed in a vacuum (**c**).

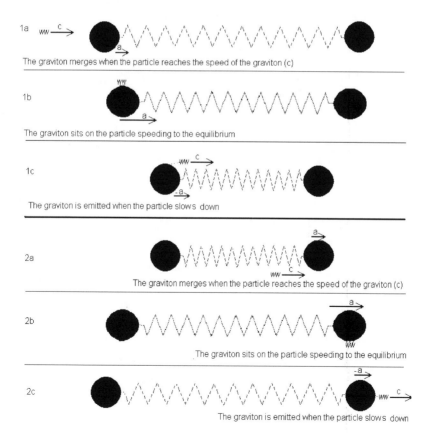

After passing the equilibrium, the particle slows down, and so emits the graviton.

If nuclear particles cause gravitons to speed up, then in accordance with the Newton's third law (which states that the mutual forces of action and reaction between two bodies are equal, opposite, and collinear), a graviton should push the associated particle in an opposite direction. That is, the graviton will push the met particle in the direction of the object emitting the gravitons, i.e. the graviton source.

The object pulls gravitons and so the gravitons pull the object to their source

Since the met object must also emit gravitons, these, reaching the first object, pull it to *their* source.

The mass of an object is essentially the sum of the masses of the protons and neutrons comprising the object, so the density of interacting gravitons is proportionate to the mass of the object. This density of emitted gravitons falls as the distance from their source increases, such that the attractive force, **F**, is proportionate to the mass of the first object, m_1, and to the mass of the second object, m_2, and disproportionate to the distance between them, **r**, where **G** is the universal gravitational constant.

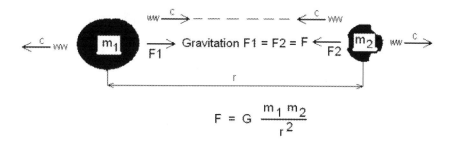

$$F = G \frac{m_1 m_2}{r^2}$$

This is Newton's law of universal gravitation: Every point mass in the universe attracts every other point mass with a force that is directly proportional to the product of their masses and inversely proportional to the square of the distance between them. If this gravitational force (**F**) is stable, then a lighter object accelerates (**a**) per Newton's Second Law of Motion (**F = ma**). Earthly beings have mass less than the mass of the Earth and, therefore, are bound to the Earth. Our movement from the Earth's surface can have fatal consequences, because our return must be by accelerating toward the Earth (falling freely).

People lack any ability to interact directly with gravitons, because God has created us through the principle of photons and electromagnetic energy (Genesis 1:3). That is why we are unable to prove their existence, e.g., to detect gravitons, and so they remain hypothetical particles. Since gravitons are born from vibration, they exhibit, besides the properties of particles, the property of waves as well. These waves are longitudinal traveling waves; and because they are waves, they bear information about the source. To catch information carried by traveling longitudinal waves, we need membranes, like the basilar membrane in the ear. This could not apply to God, because the Being of the Throne has many membranes or wings (Revelation 4:8).

Spirits in flesh (human beings) are simply bound to the Earth by the gravitational force (Job 38:6). Since gravitons carry this force, in order to be released from this bondage, we must not collide with gravitons (of the Earth). To accomplish this, we must have a perfect flesh—and thus, the eternal flesh. The city itself should not produce any gravitons and thus should not interfere with gravitons, and so was not created in Creation of the Universe. Its stones should be clear as crystal (Revelation 21:11).

Charged protons and electrons inside atoms are the sources of electromagnetic force. The proton and the electron are the fundamental particles of the universe, and they are bound by the attractive Coulomb force. The proton is positive and the electron negative. Since the proton is 1,836 times heavier than the electron, the proton forces the lighter electron to orbit around it. The Coulomb force pulls the electron toward the proton; and the centrifugal force, due to the kinetic energy of the electron, pulls the proton toward the electron. Since we live, this tension must decline through some form of work that frees entropy (e.g., heat at some temperature). Hence, some parts of the electron are emitted. Science names these particles photons.

A photon tends to move at a constant velocity along a straight line. Photons are generated by circular movement (the electron orbiting the proton and the spin of the electron) and, therefore, we register them as transverse waves. They generate electromagnetic waves, carrying basic information about their source. We have spherical eyes to register the information that they carry (intensity and color). The Being of the Throne has many eyes (Ezekiel 10:12) to see everything.

If stranger photons meet electrons moving in the same direction (velocity vector), they may merge due to the principles of electromagnetism. In merging, some force must influence the photon to change direction from a straight line to circular movement. This contact force must be directed toward the center, and thus to the proton, in order to give centripetal acceleration to the photon. As the proton, via the electron, exerts force on the photon, the photon must exert the same force in an opposite direction on the electron. This merging moves the electron to a higher orbit, or energy level. Since such an excited atomic state must also break, the electron in such a state should decay by emitting another photon.

When light advances through transparent matter, the emission should occur after a full 360-degree orbital period around any atom encountered, since light advances through transparent matter invariably in the original direction. This precludes any partial orbit—e.g., 45 degrees, 90 degrees, or 270 degrees. Experimental observations of light propagated through transparent materials, such as glass or air, reveal that light moves more slowly through these materials than it does through a vacuum. Since the speed of light is constant, then the observed speed of light in transparent materials must be less due to the changed trajectories. The described absorption and re-emission of photons should have such a trajectory:

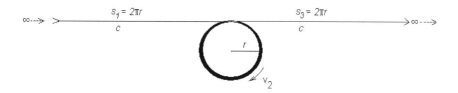

You may notice that the photon did not move forward during the time taken to complete an orbit, i.e., during the orbital period.

The Law of Conservation of Momentum requires that the momentum of our object (proton or electron) and the momentum of the photon before merging must be equal to momentum of merging. If the mass of the photon entering the collision is **m** and the mass of our object is **M**, the Law of Conservation of Momentum means:

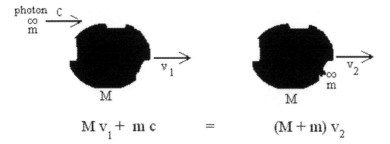

$$M v_1 + m c \quad = \quad (M + m) v_2$$

then the velocity of our object during merging v_2:

$$v_2 = \frac{M v_1}{M + m} + \frac{m c}{M + m}$$

If our object did not move before collision $v_1 = 0$,
then it moves during merging by the speed:

$$v_2 = \frac{m c}{M + m}$$

where $m c = \dfrac{h}{\lambda}$
- Planck constant
- wavelength

Thus, it is clear that photons do not attract objects. I have proven instead that photons push objects, causing them to move in their own direction. Since the electron takes some time (**T**) to complete an orbit, then the object is displaced for the distance **s = Tv$_2$** during that orbital period. If photons also interact with matter, then we do not need any hypothetical dark energy in order to explain the expansion of the universe.

Photons are bound, practically, to electrons displaced to orbits far from the associated atomic nuclei. Since electrons produce the strong electromagnetic field, photons are forced to stop on the surfaces of atoms and molecules. They act only on that surface. This can be observed from the action of light, which hardly passes through most matter, although matter is mostly empty space (just like the rest of the universe). That is why we typically see just the surfaces of objects in visible light and, with a few exceptions, do not see through them. Therefore, the repulsive force carried by photons is not applicable on objects composed of heavier atoms and molecules. This is in contrary to the gravitational force, which needs the atoms and molecules of planets, moons, comets, asteroids, and older stars in order to be significant. Gravitation needs bound protons that come into existence through the thermonuclear fusion of hydrogen in a star's core.

In the beginning of the universe, particles such as protons and neutrons (baryons) came into being. They were bound in pairs; and so the gravitational force came to exist, as I described earlier. Besides the baryons, electrons come into being as well, and bound themselves to protons due to their electric charges. And so, the first ordinary hydrogen came into existence.

The hot, dense cores of stars create energy through the fusion of atomic nuclei. Mostly, photons carry this energy away from the stars. Therefore the repulsive force pushing the universe apart depends upon the luminosity of stars, novae, and supernovae. Photons push hydrogen away; so, they push apart mostly hydrogen clouds or stars at their births. Hence, the repulsive effect also depends upon the amount of hydrogen in an object.

Stars die when they are unable to fuse new nuclei in their cores. Since we live in this part of the universe, where many stars have burned out to form heavier nuclei, the gravitational attraction is dominant in our surroundings. Where new stars are formed, photons dominate; and therefore, the expansion of the universe rules there.

In general, some force should cause all the movement in the universe. That force can act to push or to pull. Naturally, these two forces should both exist in the universe. If gravitons mediate pulling (attraction), then photons should mediate pushing (repulsion).

When the inhabitants of the New Jerusalem need to change location, the city may be relocated easily, because its placement does not depend on either gravitons (a gravitational force) or photons (a repulsive force). Since the Lamb is going to move on to the Earth, his Wife should follow Him; and so, the New Jerusalem will eventually move to the Earth. *"And he carried me away in the Spirit to a mountain great and high, and showed me the Holy City, Jerusalem, coming down out of Heaven from God"* (Revelation 21:10).

Resurrected humans, grouped as a body under the name of the Wife of the Lamb, will move with God the Son (their Husband) to the Earth. *"I saw Heaven standing open and there before me was a White Horse, whose rider is called Faithful and True. The armies of Heaven were following him, riding on white horses and dressed in fine linen, white and clean"* (Revelation 19:11-14). They are dressed in clean white linen, and so they cannot be returning from battles or other commitments. Therefore the armies of Heaven following Him are not angels of God the Father, but recruits just enrolled in God's Army.

Humans are also God's servants, because when John intended to worship the angel, the angel said to him: *"Do not do it! I am a fellow servant with you and with your brothers who hold to the testimony of Jesus. Worship God!"* (Revelation 19:10). This means that humans will serve God after the Wedding banquet just as angels once did. By this point, after the breaking the Seventh Seal, the angels should be busy with affairs of the wars and the harvesting of the earth. Our recruits enter the story in the Seventh Seal; indeed, they got their commissions just for the finale of the Heavenly Book. Those riding on white were charged with the task during the Wedding of the Lamb (Revelation 19:9), which is why are still as in their wedding robes (fine linen, white and clean).

The result of their expedition is the final destruction of the evildoers, and the rescue of those who have been left behind. The recruits were already performing this task in flesh, when they used the sword of God's word. At that time, they believed that God's servants were nearby to save them in all situations. Now, they themselves are going to save and render aid to other believers in God.

The inhabitants of the Earth should not be able to see them, just as we do not see angels. They should recognize God in Christ Jesus; the Messiah has saved them from evildoers, so He should be praised, not the resurrected humans. The recruits act following the words of God the Son: *"Out of his mouth comes a sharp sword with which to strike down the nations. He will rule them with an iron scepter"* (Revelation 19:15).

The Lamb may enter the material world as He did first when he revealed Himself to Abraham, like the Mighty Angel making decisions about Sodom and Gomorrah. He must show Himself as the Coming Messiah. He will not dwell in palaces or any other habitation but the Temple itself.

The Lord enters Jerusalem

The Earth is the first to welcome Him. The Mount of Olives will split open to form a very great valley; half the mountain will be moved to the north, and half of it to the south (Zechariah 14:4). Then 144,000 Redeemed will welcome the Messiah and *"follow the Lamb wherever he goes. They were purchased from among men, and offered as first fruits to God and the Lamb"* (Revelation 14:4). The people of Jerusalem will see the One who was wounded by their hands, pierced; their grief for Him will be bitter, like the grief of one sorrowing for his oldest son. In that day there will be a great weeping in Jerusalem (Zechariah 12:10-14).

The power will take those awaiting Him for so long, those 144,000 who were sealed away and kept safe for this hour. The Lamb will be the King of the material world through them, just as He was the King of Israel before they choose a man to be their king (1 Samuel 8:7). The 144,000 will work for the new order on the Earth, until others take their places or until they die. One of them will be a prince of the government, probably a prime minister.

The Messiah will enter the Temple using the gate facing east. He will not return to the material world again. *"Son of Man, this* [the Temple] *is the place of my throne and the place for the soles of my feet. This is where I will live among the Israelites forever"* (Ezekiel 43:1-7). The outer gate of the Sanctuary, the one facing east, "remains shut. It must not be opened; no one may enter through it. It is to remain shut because the LORD, the God of Israel, has entered through it. The Prince himself is the only one who may sit inside the gateway to eat in the presence of the LORD" (Ezekiel 44:1-4). I understand this to mean that the governor of the world will come to the Temple for advice from God. Thus, he would talk to Him face to face like Moses did.

Hence, "the name of the city from that time on will be: THE LORD IS THERE" (Ezekiel 48:35). Nations should go to worship Him there. *"If any of the people of the earth do not go up to Jerusalem to worship the King, the Lord almighty, they will have no rain"* (Zechariah 14:17).

Viewed from another angle, the impact of the Millennium is that no evil powers will be allowed to afflict Creation for a thousand years. Therefore, the angels should bind them for this period; in a sense, the evil powers shall be put in jail (Revelation 20:1-3). The angels are able to do this now because the recruits come to occupy the territory which was their previous battlefield (or working place).

In any case, beings in the likeness of angels must inhabit the invisible world of the Earth. These new beings are *"those who had been beheaded because of their testimony for Jesus and because of the word of God. They had not worshiped the beast or his image and had not received his mark on their foreheads or their hands. They came to life and reigned with Christ a thousand years"* (Revelation 20:4-6). Now they take the territory where evil forces once had their bastions. The invisible world is their booty. There, the Wife of the Lamb will work.

The resurrected humans could not exist in the material world to live with their families in Earthly flesh, because they have forever left that existence, based on declining, or increasing entropy. According to the Second Law of Thermodynamic, everything in the universe moves, not toward evolution but toward death. (Death will be destroyed at the end of created things, after the Millennium—Revelation 20:14.)

Photons carry away electromagnetic energy. The radiation is spread by waves having different wavelengths, producing the entire spectrum of electromagnetic radiation. Created humans are hung on this radiation; they move in photons. Part of the spectrum warms us; some hurts us; and some transfers information (e.g., TV, radio, and cell phone signals). We see by means of part of the range of the electromagnetic spectrum. Light is electromagnetic radiation that we see; it is the range in which the sun emits most of its radiation. On Earth, the deficit of energy caused by the Second Law of Thermodynamics—lost through natural disorganization—is substituted by the energy coming from the sun. If the sun ever burns out, the Earth's will die.

The existence of the Wife does not depend on the energy coming from the sun: "*. . . and showed me the Holy City, Jerusalem, coming down out of heaven from God. It shone with the glory of God, and its brilliance was like that of a very precious jewel, like a jasper, clear as crystal. The city does not need the sun or the moon to shine on it, for the glory of God gives it light, and the Lamb is its lamp* (Revelation 21:10-11, 23). So, Earthly beings move in photons; but beings of the New Jerusalem move in God, move in God's light. God could not be compared with the sun, which will someday burn out. God is the Eternal, and so these moving in His light live eternal life.

Earthly beings see by means of photons, so we are unable to see others who do not absorb and reemit or emit photons. That is why created humans are unable to see angels and spirits in our normal surroundings. This leads to the conclusion that people still in flesh during the Millennium will not see the Wife of the Lamb.

The next difference is in gravity. If gravitons could affect the Wife of the Lamb, then their Wedding would have had to be on the Earth; it could not be in the Heaven. Similarly, the New Jerusalem would have been built on two-dimensional area and not in three-dimensional space, as we know in fact it was; it is described as being as wide and high as it is long. If the Lamb and His Wife were to return to live in the material world, to them it would be like living in a jail. Why would God sentence them for something wrong done after the Resurrection, that they should be jailed by gravity?

Beings of the material world can communicate only if they can produce vibrant waves in some medium. Hearing comes from our perception of longitudinal waves—compressions and rarefaction of the air. However, this could not occur in a vacuum, and thus could not occur in space, in which people are raptured, or in Heaven. Men visiting Heaven testify (and I also) that communication does not occur There in the same way it does during our life in flesh. Words are put inside another's head without any vibration occurring. The speed of sound is very small in the material world, compared with a speed of thought, with which God communicates with angels.

To venture into the spiritual field, then, Earthly beings of the Millennium will be connected to God through the Temple. The spiritual healing will occur in the Temple. Priests will serve the people, and help them to live a holy life. Ezekiel speaks of the Temple services, as does Zechariah: "*In that day a fountain will be opened to the house of David and to the people of Jerusalem, to cleanse them from sin and impurity*" (Zechariah 13:1).

God needs to heal the material world as well; this healing will also come from the Temple, because waters will flow from the Temple and into the sea. "*When it empties into the sea, the water there becomes fresh. Swarms of living creatures will live wherever the river flows. There will be large numbers of fish, because this water flows there and makes the salt water fresh; so where the river flows everything will live.*" "*Fruit trees of all kinds will grow on both banks of the river. Their leaves will not wither, nor will their fruit fail. Every month they will bear, because the water from the sanctuary flows to them. Their fruit will serve for food and their leaves for healing*" (Ezekiel 47 and Zechariah 14).

The Wife will live with God (the Lamb). "He will wipe every tear from their eyes. There will be no more death or mourning or crying or pain, **for the old order of things has passed away**" (Revelation 21:4). The Marriage occurs on the Earth, and should last a thousand years. During this time, people of the material world will be born and die. The Wife will supervise them. At the end of the Millennium, the earth will be overpopulated; and then everything that was created will come to an end. This is because the Earth was not intended to support created life forever. Life depends on the sun, and the sun cannot shine forever. According to our understanding of the life cycle of the Sun, its next phase should be the Red Giant. During this state, "the light of the moon will be as the light of the sun, and the light of the sun will be seven times greater, as the light of seven days." This is detailed in Isaiah 30: 25-33. I believe the Red Giant phase is the Lake of Fire mentioned in the Bible.

God will disconnect the New Jerusalem from the Earth when the Lake of Fire comes into being. The New Jerusalem will move on to a new Earth, one not having any sea and having another sky (Revelation 21:1). Taken literally, this suggests that another celestial body elsewhere in Universe will be our new home. If that is the case, we still will not live mortal lives there.

The Bible describes our destiny after the Millennium in Revelation 22:1-5.

I see the Kingdom of God the Father described there. During the Millennium (and so, the Marriage), the throne of God will be in the Temple, and the River of Life (or simply water) will flow out from the Temple. But this will not be so in the Kingdom of God the Father.

Then the angel showed me the river of the water of life, as clear as crystal, flowing from the throne of God and of the Lamb. God the Father (God) and God the Son (the Lamb) are together on the Throne and, therefore, they are in the Kingdom of God in Heaven.

His servants *will see his face, and his name will be on their foreheads.* I conclude, then, that by this point the Marriage has ended, and the next stage is our relationship to God the Father, because we will bear His name in our job. If we will be His servants, we may see His face also then.

In the words of the Apostle Paul, "then the end will come when he hands over the Kingdom to God the Father . . . then the Son himself will be made subject to him who put everything under him, so that God may be all in all" (1 Corinthians 15:24-28).

Conclusion

We did not know our Father in Heaven, and so He found us by sending His Son. We may acknowledge Him even more as we advance through the three stages of our relationship to His Son. A result of this relationship is, we will enter an eternal relationship with God and His Throne in Heaven.

Whoever does not acknowledge the Savior has not stepped onto the path to Heaven. Whoever does not enter into a spiritual relationship or love with the Savior is not the member of the Church. Certainly, the Church itself is not the Bride of the Lamb. The Lamb will come for her to be His Bride. Also, the Church is not the Wife of the Lamb if she does not go through the wedding ceremony in Heaven.